Susanne Lehmann

Team leadership in the real world

Stories about leadership

Text: © Copyright by Susanne Lehmann
Cover design© Copyright by Susanne Lehmann
Publisher:
Susanne Lehmann,
Okerstraße 13,
51371 Leverkusen
Susanne.Lehmann@miteinanderbusiness.com

Table of contents

Introduction 4

First steps 5

Minijob 8

Between the chairs 13

Too much of a good thing 21

Everything back to square one.....................26

Recognition and bullying.............................35

A little factory 42

Subordinate of a workaholic 51

From the rain to the eaves...........................61

Short and sweet 70

Cold water...79

Time witnesses..89

Conclusion:..98

My advice:...99

About me 103

Introduction

I would like to share my experiences as a former employee in the cleaning and security industry, which I have made myself and learned from them.

Maybe I can give one or the other thought-provoking impulse, maybe I can also make sure that one can sleep well again or prevent the earth-shattering feelings of anger and helplessness.

Nothing of what I write is scientifically provable, it should only serve to not make the same mistakes or to learn a little more.

No names will be mentioned, not that I am afraid of consequences, but I am subject to privacy as well as personal respect.

Everything I tell, I have personally experienced. Nothing is second hand or made up.

First steps

Everyone started working at some point, somewhere, anything. My favorite start was at a company where I was the youngest building cleaning employee in my mid-twenties. I felt as if I were a teenager just out of school. I had to be taught everything, systems had to be explained, procedures had to be internalized, and in some cases I had to be taken to the exit because I kept getting lost in these objects. It was no fun for my colleagues, but they put up with it for a while.

The forewomen were mentors for all who needed and wanted it. They didn't just observe, but gave tips, really worked ahead, and even lent a hand themselves. I was very impressed by that and learned a lot during that time.

Friendliness and a sense of humor go a long way with employees, and a certain amount of composure at work also takes the pressure off your own nerves. Even though I was the new one, people talked to me so that they could get to know each other better. Interest was shown in what I had to tell, and people laughed together. Stories were told from the time when I wasn't there and they were really funny. It wasn't always just about work, but we talked about everyday things, as if we were standing at the bakery waiting to buy some rolls.

I had been in the service industry for a while and the customers were much more relaxed in their ways than they are today. People always worked hard, only back then work was still work and free time was still free time. Breaks were taken in other rooms, and everyone still took their breaks. We met with our colleagues and spent time together. Today, when I see how rushed many people are through their lives, I realize how much calmer work was back then.

There were also tactics for time management, which is not a new invention. The bosses of those days were more relaxed, even though there was no super developed internet, email traffic or inter-net conferences. In my early days, I was totally intimidated when the boss was still in the house, until I realized he was also just people with a family and a home.

At that time, I didn't perceive the responsibility that a leader should have, nor did I have anything to do with all of this. Now I know that it takes a lot of expertise to deal with your teams like that as a leader. Psychology already played a role back then, active listening was practiced back then, the agile way of working was also always present. When I look at it from my perspective today, we haven't reinvented the wheel. We just learned, un-learned and remembered again.

My daughter was the reason for the end of my work there. A move to another location also made it impossible for me to return there at that time.

I owe a lot to the ladies of that time, including the fact that I am now as I am.

Minijob

In a job ad in the daily newspaper, a cleaner was wanted for the morning hours. My daughter went to kindergarten and my sons to school. From the working hours, it fits wonderfully to find a way back into working life after my parental leave.

I introduced myself and got the job.

I was trained with the colleague from the late shift, after three days I said I was ready and the forewoman was also there in the morning to do her job. If there were any questions, I knew where to find her.

The operation was dirty, the procedures were always the same, so I couldn't do much wrong. The staff was satisfied and also saw when something was left undone. Of course, they made up for it, since the weekly schedule was such that there was the opportunity to do so.

One fine day, we received a visit from the object management, who brought us new employment contracts. There was a wage increase coming up and we were all supposed to sign that our hours were being cut.

My 3-hour position was cut to 2.15 hours. The procedures were to remain the same. I brought this up and the property manager said that it was calculated in the office on the square footage of my precinct. When I told her about the time it took to get from A to B, she just said that the instructions came from above.

We, as colleagues, agreed that we would first have a look at the new times and then have another talk.

As I was alone with my forewoman on the early shift, I had told her several times that I would not be able to cope with the work or that I was leaving the company with overtime that no one was paying me. She went with me once and said it would be fine with time. When I asked when the object manager would come again, she wanted to let me know.

Another four weeks must have passed. During that time, complaints started to come in.

When I talked to the employees and told them what had happened, they could only shake their heads. They agreed with me that the time was no longer manageable and complained to the management. The goal was actually to get more time out for all of us. What none of us knew was that the contract had been put out to tender. That's why there was no more response from the upper floor.

I called the property manager myself and described my situation to her. She was surprised at my statement, since the forewoman had always maintained that everything had been in order. She had never said a word about my complaints. We made an appointment and surprised the forewoman with the visit of the object management. The two of them had a lot to say to each other.

Then they got to talking about my concerns. The forewoman wanted to give me a little more time to get used to the new situation, was her answer. The object management had brought the precinct plans with them, on which one could see exactly the procedures and square meterage of the duty rosters. The walking routes were not considered, which could have been changed, was the statement afterwards. Nothing was changed, because we lost the order shortly thereafter.

The next company wanted to take us over and presented us with new rosters with new working hours so that we could decide whether we would go along.

When I saw my work schedules, it was clear to me that even more time had been saved. They had taken the cheapest supplier who participated in the tender, and there was no longer any talk of quality. I didn't want to work there under these circumstances, because I knew that the complaints would pile up. After five years in this company, I already knew many workers and knew that, the trouble was already pre-programmed.

When I talked to a friend about how quickly and callously people were fired there, we both realized that this is how the world can tick. If I could have done it differently, I would have been more sensitive with the team members. We worked in the company for more than 5 years and left a lot of heart and soul there. Well, that was the way things were.

Between the chairs

I joined a medium-sized company with several departments, which hired me as a part-time cleaner. I had a fixed object to secure my working hours and was then on the road in different objects when someone went on vacation or was absent due to illness. I also drove materials out to relieve the object manager. I was given a company car and was a permanent guest in the office. There I took my first steps as a forewoman.

My permanent job was in a kitchen studio, upscale and very well-kept. My colleague, who also worked there, showed me my cleaning room and the cleaning schedule that was posted there and left me alone. She wasn't far away, just one floor below me, so I could always go to her if I had questions. For the first few days, I stumbled through my department until I found my routine.

Since we had the same work hours, we also got off work at the same time and always chatted for a few minutes before we left. I felt comfortable and even on Saturdays I got the duty done pretty well since we took turns so everyone could have a weekend off.

There were three furniture stores in the area. In a short time, I was able to work in all three, alternating Saturdays. More hours, more money, more experience, a win - win situation for everyone.

In the kitchen studio there was a very quickly promoted department manager (a colleague told me) who did not want to deal with me. I was probably too "defiant", because in his opinion, he had to explain everything. I listened to him attentively and carried out his suggestions. However, he did not want me in his house. After the incidents, I spoke with my property manager and she looked for a successor for me. I trained her and left my permanent job at the furniture stores.

In retrospect, I learned that they just didn't like me. At first, I had a hard time with it, but our boss told me in a conversation that something like that could happen. I stayed in the area as a floater and everyone was happy.

Sometimes I worked in other companies before the furniture store. This expanded my knowledge of how to deal with customers and what mistakes to make only once.

My favorite business manager, I guess he was past retirement age, once said to me, "Girl, you don't make that much mess at my age, just come back tomorrow." I was in my early forties.

This property was cleaned twice a day. The cleaner was on vacation and I had done the substitution there. In the morning, at the crack of dawn, I must have set off the audible alarm three times, because I had simply not managed to keep to the few seconds that were needed between switching off the alarm and entering the building. I once went to the company at noon to find someone who could explain to me how to do it properly. The secretary of the building, started laughing when I told her the story. She showed me how it worked and also explained to me that if I just pulled the door shut again, the alarm would go silent again. Nothing could happen, nor would the police come, since this was a twenty-four-hour operation. I thanked her and the alarm has not been an issue since.

Another boss, whom I sometimes met in the evenings, was surprised that everything was clean lately, even though the cleaner was sick. In the beginning, he hadn't seen me at all because this property was a key location and I could come as I pleased. Once he intercepted me because he couldn't reach my property manager and didn't know who else was in the facility besides his employees. We talked about the procedures, what he expected and in general. In the process, I realized that bosses can also be okay.

Sometimes they are arrogant and condescending. This boss once told me that he knew what his employees were capable of and that he would treat them with respect. I noticed that about myself, too, because he would ask me, whenever we met, how he could make my job easier. I couldn't think of anything at the time, assured him that I would get back to him if it came to that.

Another substitute position was more complicated, as it only required cleaning twice a week. My property manager just couldn't find a suitable person to take care of the property. I was there two weeks at a time until someone came in and said after the second day of work that she didn't want to do it anymore. When I took over again, the customer became impatient. I talked to my property manager and we made out that I would stay on for now to calm the customer down as well. He wasn't being rude, he just wanted someone to clean his place constantly, after all we had a contractual agreement that everyone had to abide by. It took a while to find someone who would stay. The customer was satisfied and the goal was achieved.

In the next substitute position, things were getting busy. The cleaner went on vacation. Before that, she trained me, I took over the key and I had the task of keeping everything in shape for two weeks. I usually came in during the time when the boss and his secretary were on vacation. So, we saw each other regularly and talked briefly. Sometimes I was asked to bring a job forward, and in return I had to postpone something else until the next day. I managed to comply and when the two weeks were over, there was a box of chocolates on the table. A small thank you, which I was very happy about.

Unfortunately, the cleaner fell ill a short time later and no one knew if she would return. From the experience with the small object place, we had learned. I stood in for her until she was able to return to work and that was a great success.

My property manager stopped contacting me from one day to the next and I later learned that she would be staying home for the time being. A new employee was hired. I got along very well with her at first, because she had already been a manager in the cleaning business. I showed her the properties, drove around with her, met with her to show her what was important to some customers and how we worked. I felt I was in the best possible position and gratitude actually came from her.

In between, we had construction cleaning work in various properties that were about to open. Sometimes I found myself working as a foreman with a team of at least twenty colleagues. Since almost all of us knew each other, I was able to manage the coordination well and we successfully got out of the orders.

I was also supposed to work together with the glass cleaning foreman from my new property manager position. When I made a substitution and called him that the windows needed to be cleaned again, he came and took a look.

Likewise, if there was a basic cleaning job to be done, we discussed it and it was done in no time.

I saw eye-to-eye with the last property manager, but the next one had to push me down again because our boss had reviewed the operating costs and decided that money had to be saved. For me, this meant fewer orders, only one fixed object, hardly any substitutions, and the material trips were once again the responsibility of the object management.

I had to give up my company car, I suffered financial losses and was extremely frustrated.

I would have liked to have been talked to beforehand. Basically, I was only told that I had to give up various jobs, substitute jobs were divided up differently, and the property management had to add as additional tasks that I had completed.

The only person to complain to was the owner of the company, our boss. I couldn't get into the office anymore, because my work was throttled down so much that there was no need for it.

I should have taken better care of myself contractually, but I had neglected to do so. My trust was in the word that was given to me. This did not happen to me a second time.

Too much of a good thing

I had looked for a second job and was hired as a forewoman in the cleaning department. The manager was of the opinion that I had the necessary experience. A colleague in the same position trained me in different areas. Since we needed management certificates in different buildings, I was not allowed to go out on my own for the first time. This was an advantage for me, as I learned under supervision which procedures were prescribed and who should work in which area and when.

In addition, I could already determine my later sequences and inspections of the objects. That saved me a lot of time.

After ten days, I received my confirmation and was allowed to work alone.

A colleague, who was already retired and only came to work because otherwise the ceiling would fall on her head, kept the team together. I found her knowledge of the building, the people who worked there and their stories incredibly impressive. She was the good soul in the building. Even when employers changed, she stuck up for the team. Most of the team members had been there for more than four years, which means they were almost all taken over by the company.

It is always worth mentioning that in such cases, team dynamics are very strong. When substitute work has to be done, the assignment is made in a few minutes. A feeling of injustice then rarely arises, because you can always rely on each other.

I was assigned an area in order to get my number of hours, and when I was finished there, I was supposed to check the material stock and take the used mops and other dirty laundry to the warehouse to be washed. I was on the road to relieve the property manager and I enjoyed making the interpersonal contact. This was, as I later discovered, my core competence.

In this object I learned a lot. Most of the time I just listened. I was told about the peculiarities of the agency. We had to abide by the rules of the staff. For example, we had to clean the accounting office by the end of the working day, otherwise we couldn't get in. Then a recreation room was only to be cleaned if it was really empty. Sometimes we could only clean properly on Friday afternoons, which was not so bad because it was already known.

Some office workers let the colleagues into the rooms to clean by going out of the room during that time, others said that it could be postponed to the next day. Then only the trash cans were emptied.

In my department, it was like I had to sign in and out when I entered the office. Even there, it was like you could only get into the room if someone was there. The nice thing about this whole workplace was the friendliness that came our way. Everyone on our team could look forward to friendly interactions.

My duties as a foreman actually included making changes to workflows that wouldn't fit together, only I saw no reason to do so. My project manager was satisfied and the colleagues were so well attuned.

In other objects I changed the working hours. The building cleaner always came at midday and that was not desired. The manager of the building said that it was not a problem in exceptional cases, just not in the long run, please. I spoke with the colleague and she then came in the evening at fixed times.

Working with the female colleagues and the building manager was a great time. I thought that I could make a career in this company and quit my other job. What I unfortunately realized too late was that I had worked myself into a burnout due to my two jobs.

I could no longer sleep properly and a persistent cold, with which I had already been to my family doctor, just wouldn't get better. When I sat in his treatment room again, he wrote me off sick. It is always a recommendation that a doctor can make, only the sentence "People die from your symptoms" had brought me to my senses.

I was happy in the profession. There were great people around me. My admissions were done competently and in a structured way. It gave me a secure feeling because I made few mistakes there. And if I did, the damage was usually not that great. In the times of the 90s until 2012, attention was still paid to instruction. I have the feeling that it was no longer so important after that.

Everything back to square one

After my recovery, I retrained as a security specialist and applied to a large company as a security employee.

I had not quite sent the application mail when I received an invitation for an interview. I accepted the appointment and was hired as a security guard the next day. Monday was the day to start.

On Saturday morning, I got a call from the deputy property manager, who worked the day shift, asking me if I could come by on the same day, as he wanted to discuss something with me. Two hours later, I was sitting back in the office where I was offered a job as a deputy shift manager for the night shift. The reason was that they were desperately looking for someone for this position and I, with my training, was the perfect candidate. We talked about the tasks and the associated skills and went through the objects together.

Back in the office, I said yes, since I had already had to do foreman tasks from my previous job. My work references and the reputation of my former lecturer had probably done the rest to this quick promotion.

The first few days I was on the road with the night shift supervisor, who showed me everything he knew. He explained the operational procedure, walked with me through the different objects, took care of the colleagues' needs and also showed me the office tasks that had to be done. He even made copies of pages that needed to be documented so that I could learn how to properly fill out these documents. I was impressed that I took a lot of what I learned with me for my future career.

The colleagues were great. The first shifts almost took care of themselves, I was also pointed out some things that I had almost forgotten.

Every now and then I asked why none of them would work as a deputy shift leader and then the answer came several times that they were not asked. Others did not want to and still others were not so powerful of the German language. Despite all the statements, they were all open-minded and attentive people. The work was fun, even when there were problems.

I took it upon myself to get to know everyone personally. A one-on-one conversation makes more sense than group conversations. I had the opportunity to do this because I was on the road a lot in the properties and could also help out if someone needed to use the toilet or wanted to get a coffee.

There was also no criticism of me in public. If a problem arose that needed to be solved immediately, we always found a corner where we could talk in peace. Or we went into the office, where I could close the door behind us and we were undisturbed.

With several people from different nationalities, it's not inevitable that something won't fit. Then I organized a small round of talks, where the problem could be discussed and finished. I was also able to plan personal matters, such as a day off or even a vacation at short notice, and this was well received by my colleagues.

If someone overslept, which was rarely the case, this colleague was greeted with loud welcoming calls. None of us had a bad word to say about it, unlike on the day shift. That was a different caliber.

My people skills were enhanced, each conversation I went back over for myself afterwards to see if I could have done better and what to look for in the next one.

I also made my mistakes by putting two colleagues together who could not work together. They had been complaining, and I was then given the appropriate advice. I met with the object manager between two shifts. He told me how he dealt with such situations. That same evening, I apologized for my behavior to my colleagues. After a conversation, each of us was able to continue working again with a good feeling. For me as a team leader, it was important to rectify the unpleasant situation. They are really great people who actually forgave me for this misstep.

One colleague felt unnoticed by her superiors and colleagues because she actually seemed rather unimpressive. Time and again, there were arguments when she was around. I also had a conversation with her and learned that she had a relationship with several colleagues one after the other. It was none of my business, but she felt she was no longer being taken seriously. I offered her to contact me if she got into a situation again that might have gone wrong so I could give an evaluation. It turned out that she believed that the whole world would judge her for what had happened. So she would argue with anyone who looked at her askance. As I assessed each situation, she became calmer and more relaxed because I showed her that her colleagues were not attacking her as she thought they were.

I, who live in Western Europe, have never had to think about the fact that there are mentalities that are not to be taken for granted. Some of my colleagues had difficulties accepting me as a boss at first, because they were not used to a woman giving instructions. I was impatient with them and dismissed it as disrespect when they became rude, and I treated my colleagues accordingly. It was not fair to let my tone become stricter, to be only very curt when they addressed me, or to simply disregard them during the break where we occasionally met. My posture also changed around them, as I noticed later. They were doing their jobs, but they also let me know that they didn't want to be talked to like that. I sought to talk to my object leader and exchanged ideas with him. Since he had been working with them for a long time and had also taken several courses in integration teaching, it was easy for him to explain to me how I should best proceed.

Over the next few days, I talked with each colleague in private and asked how we should interact with each other. Each one assured me that they respected me, only they felt I did not. I explained to them that they were just like any other person on earth to me and I had never seen it that way. They only wanted me to show them the respect that I also expected from them. I had not done that by my kind. We agreed on more mindfulness (even if we expressed it differently), and since that day we relaxed again.

Since we were a motley bunch, we argued, laughed and made fun of each other every now and then, until the day came when things got serious.

Everyone who had started working at the properties knew that time at the place was limited. We all had a written promise that we would be transferred if we wanted to and would be made an offer when the time came. The time to close the facility was approaching and we had not heard anything yet.

During the day shift, colleagues from another area came for a few days to help out when necessary and moved on. They did not have a permanent job. I learned from them that some jobs had already been advertised, which we knew nothing about. The temporary colleagues only knew about it because they were on the road so much and were always asked if they didn't want to stay. The other colleagues on the day shift had no idea either. Only the object manager and the shift supervisor knew about it because they were very good friends with the store manager. I approached both of them about it and was then able to find the jobs with research work.

Unfortunately, the good times we had passed. Everyone was disappointed with the company, as I guess they had forgotten about us. We talked about how to proceed now and I suggested to write a collective application of our team. The idea was particularly well received by our foreign colleagues.

Beforehand, I had contacted the responsible department manager and exchanged ideas with him. I ignored his excuse that there was still time; my colleagues were more important now. The idea of a collective advertising came from me and he accepted it. All colleagues got an interview and another employment contract for the new objects, if they wanted.

Unfortunately, there was nothing suitable for me. I applied to another company and moved to another city.

My work with my colleagues was great. At the beginning it was difficult, because my position was not clear to anyone. Within a few days, however, things eased up because I had had many conversations with my colleagues at the time and they accepted me for who I was.

Through my professional career in building cleaning, I have always had to deal with a lot of people and I enjoyed it. I was happy when we got together. There was always something new to learn and to accumulate. It was no different here. Besides spending time on shifts, we were able to get to know and trust each other.

Recognition and bullying

I ended up working in a large industrial plant for a while. I had the illusion that the security industry would play a major role in my life. As it turned out, this was not a good idea. I was to slip from one cata-strophe into the next.

I was traveling with a colleague whose job it was to show me around the plant, familiarize me with regulations, prepare documentation and secure the danger zone in the event of a plant alarm. His knowledge was enormous and since I write a lot down, he also gave me the time to do so. We walked through several buildings, switched on and off various alarm systems, unlocked and closed doors. Object inspections served to see that there was no water damage, that the emergency exits were not blocked and that no person needed help. In the late evening hours, we met isolated employees from the plant. They work with countries whose time difference was large and therefore an online conference sometimes took place at night. We drove around the site to make sure there was no damage to the fence and eight hours were gone.

The whole thing went on in different shifts for eight days and then I sat alone in the car and got my own territory. I was told over and over again that the familiarization work was too short, so I should definitely call for help if I needed any. I did, I think far too often, because after a while, I was asked if I was the right employee for the job.

We had alternating shift supervisors, with different duties. One of them apologized a few weeks after I started that he didn't have the time to train me personally. He was responsible for the paperwork. That seemed strange to me. Did that mean that he had sent our colleague off even though it wasn't his job?

Another shift supervisor dropped everything when I couldn't do my job at the plant because it wasn't shown to me. He was a nice person, just quickly annoyed. He was responsible for the reporting system.

Someone else, at the beginning of the shift, asked which precinct one wanted to take over, and then we picked one out. He knew the plant very well and in all areas of responsibility he was the master. Since he was only a substitute, he had the task of checking our report.

The youngest shift supervisor was a little weasel, extremely fast on his feet and very intelligent. He fired the instructions through the radio and was virtually on the spot by the time we got to where we were supposed to go. His goal was advanced training and he needed the hands-on experience as a shift supervisor.

I was also offered the opportunity to apply as a shift supervisor, but first I had to get to know the plant and the tasks involved.

I felt that I had quickly found my feet, my questions became fewer, I performed my tasks precisely and also received praise and recognition from colleagues, shift supervisors and the plant manager.

But then something changed, I was bullied.

It took a while before I noticed it personally. I had worked in different shifts with my colleagues and this was always mixed up among us employees. The duty roster changed monthly or weekly, and if someone got sick, it could be hourly.

Pointed comments flew across the meeting table, at first we laughed about it, until I hit a hurdle during an object inspection and asked for help. The reporting shift supervisor came on the scene and brought the colleague who had been making fun of me at the duty meetings. He made snide remarks, and I explained that I had found every door in the building, but the alarm could not be set. Almost at the end of the shift I was told that everyone had already stood in front of this building and asked for help. Not a nice situation, but I did not give up.

The colleague I had the familiarization with became extremely condescending to me. He had also taken over as the substitute shift leader and kept challenging me with special tasks. Most of them I was familiar with, but he knew better and let me run into the wall with full force. Once he thought I was too stupid to put a combination of numbers in the right order, even though I had witnesses who testified that everything was correct. It did not matter; a report went to our object leader.

Some colleagues got along better with each other and so I was spied on. They asked me if I would come with them to the break and then they told me that I had overstayed it. Another time, I came back from break and saw a colleague looking at his watch.

Two of us were called on an alarm and a colleague got in between. On the same shift, the property manager got an email claiming I didn't show up for the alarm, so the colleague had to jump in.

A large-scale operation lasted all night. I passed on my duty to the next shift. I had reported everything that still had to be dealt with in the shift and asked whether I should explain or tell anything else. This was denied. Two days later, our property manager sat in our office and asked to speak with me.

The reporting shift supervisor was sitting at the table with me, and they explained the situation to me. They praised me for being so strong in the beginning and unfortunately my performance got worse and worse. I was close to tears and told them about my view of things.

My performance had really declined, as I became more and more insecure the more I was put through this. Even the representatives of the client had noticed that my colleagues were not collegial. They told publicly about my missteps. Some colleagues had tried to protect me, only too much had gone wrong that they no longer wanted to pay attention to it.

Our object leader made me the offer of the transfer, assured me that he would also speak with the responsible colleagues and I would get a result.

Before this transfer took place, I already had another job in sight.

A new colleague told me about his old company, gave me the name of the contact person and I changed to a new adventure.

I firmly resolved to contact my superiors if something like this should happen again. Such hostility was foreign to me. All of a sudden, I was so sensitized that it was difficult for me to gain trust in my new job. Normally, I am an open person who allows new things to happen. For some time, my new colleagues had a really hard time with me. At some point, with consideration for the old colleagues who had stood by me, I told my story and was advised that there would be extra training for this as part of a continuing education program. Every manager should take part in it, that was the idea.

The situation or a similar one did not happen again in my case.

A little factory

With a duty roster, new work clothes, a bottle of water and some nerve food, I stood in front of the revolving door that led into the small factory. Somehow, I didn't want to, because the last workplace had already left its mark on me. But now it was no use. Just one small step and I was already standing in the foyer of the reception area in the plant where I was going to work as a security guard.

You could already tell by my clothes that I belonged. It was shift handover, a lot of colleagues were standing behind the counter talking. One of them looked at me, open look, smile, positive posture, of-fen hands. He extended one of them to me, introduced himself and told me to come to the back. We were all on a first-name basis. First names flew towards me and we greeted each other with a handshake.

In the next moment the flying exchange was initiated. Some left, others stayed and another one of them drove me to my workstation.

I entered a construction container, where a counter was built in, behind it a table with two chairs, monitor, keyboard, mouse and trays on top. Then a time clock, forms and more trays. The assistant property manager sat on a chair and greeted me.

We were at a truck entrance. There were gate guards outside, checking IDs, instructing truck drivers, sending strangers in and handing us IDs through the window. It was a real hustle and bustle. My colleague was totally relaxed and worked through everything. Two hours later it was quiet.

I was dizzy just from watching. My colleague laughed and explained to me that things would not normally be so hectic. There were several construction sites in the plant. The outside workers were given passes that they could use for a week, and because it was Monday, it was also busy. In fact, on Mondays all hell broke loose and the rest of the week you had to bring your own employment, at least at the truck entrances.

I spent ten days being trained in different areas and on different shifts. I got to know some of my colleagues for a short time, because they would let themselves be seen at the different gates when they were on a plant tour.

We talked a lot, I learned about previous stories with their bosses and colleagues, and when I told them which plant I had worked in before, many of them laughed and said that they worked here too, but nowhere near as hectic as elsewhere. A wellness oasis in the area of plant security. In the course of time, I also had a look at the various gates, it was part of the job. The property manager also worked like this. When he wasn't in the office, he spent time with us. Being close to his people was important to him. Before his promotion, he had worked at the plant himself.

The previous object manager was quietly removed after a disastrous mishap. A new one had to be found in a hurry. And the new property manager was a true encyclopedia about the plant, a master in protection and security and had an incomprehensible general knowledge.

He promised one-on-one meetings, for which I had to wait a bit, but then he took his time. I took it upon myself to report many good experiences about colleague, because he asked how I had been treated.

Of course, I also got into trouble with my colleagues, but he knew his friends, so I didn't tell anything new anyway.

There are jibes everywhere, and it was nowhere near as bad as in the first work. Even in gender-balanced professional partnerships, there are quarrels or injustice, so everything was good here. On the whole, every single colleague tried to share his or her knowledge. Somehow it was already a power struggle, if several together told about experiences. Details were discussed heatedly, since everyone had a different perception. If one is longer present, it can become funny to observe the cockfights.

It was about four weeks before the end of my probationary period when I was driving through the plant with my then object manager. I asked him what he thought of my performance and he was pleased. When I pointed out to him that my probationary period was about to end, he just said very dryly that he could take his time with the evaluation until the last day. Why he said that, I didn't know, it didn't leave a good feeling.

A few days later, we all received mail from the accounting office, telling us to please fill in our vacation days and that no vacation would be taken into the new year, exceptions would have to be submitted in writing. As mentioned, I was still in my probationary period.

Our property manager also came to me and wanted my vacation slip in two days so he could plan. I complied with his request and my vacation was approved. I was looking forward to it, planning to go away for a few days, and as if he had guessed, he called me after my booking confirmation and asked if I could still postpone the vacation.

A colleague who came to the plant before me had been relieved of duty during his shift shortly beforehand and then resigned. No one could say what had happened. Everything happened during his probationary period.

I wanted to keep my job, so I postponed my vacation, I rebooked, and when I realized that I would be out of town when my probationary period expired, I figured I would just have to find a new job when I got back.

When I came back from my vacation, I was still employed. So, I went on duty as usual, was told what had happened, and things went on as normal until just before Christmas.

There were some colleagues who were fighting over the holidays and others didn't want to have anything to do with it. I didn't care, I had requested one day of Christmas for "off" and it went through.

The hook at the history, it was emergency service. No one knew why, and no one could explain it. A freak of nature? No, just stricter rules that our project manager pulled out of his hat. A colleague had contacted the area manager and the on-call service was broken up, as I later learned. Here, too, we didn't always work with the same colleagues, so we didn't always find out everything immediately.

In the new year, new requirements came from the customer and we were trained for all we were worth. Our property manager was also involved and you could see how pale and thin he had become.

We had to document everything that was possible. Sometimes we sat at work tables and wrote endless reports. The rumor that we were losing the contract went around.

What I am telling you now was not clear to me in that situation. I understood it only later.

All of a sudden, everything happened very quickly.

Our object manager drew up duty rosters that hardly contained any rest periods.

Out of five-night shifts, we had one day off so that we could come in for the early shift the next day. In between, there were always twelve-hour shifts, so that all the workplaces were occupied.

At noon, calls came in asking if you should come in early for the night shift because someone had dropped out. During the shift, people asked if they could work longer.

Shortly before the end of the night shift, there were instructions to stay late because a colleague did not show up for work.

The tone became rougher, hardly anyone was willing to communicate with colleagues, some got sick and the rest of the staff worked their hearts out.

Different shifts meant different sleep patterns, stress on the body, physical ailments, mental and physical strain. Especially when there are no longer regular working hours and you only go home to sleep, it happened that you were not concentrated and could, for example, put yourself in mortal danger in traffic, no longer eat sensibly, become irritable and mean towards other people and in the end collapse.

I know from some colleagues that they have been taking medication for years to keep up with the stress, from others I have heard that they have died from it. Still others claim that security guards don't grow old, especially those on the night shift are hit hard.

I almost had an accident and circulatory collapse on the way home twice during a shift. The company doctor sent me home and my family doctor recommended therapeutic time off. My foray into the security industry was over.

The property was later transferred to another service company. The new prerequisites issued by the plant management at the beginning of 2018 were available for the management to see. Even a master of protection and security reaches his limits. He was given the task of employee leadership when he was promoted from plant security employee to plant property manager. He had no experience in leadership, perhaps his pride got in the way, but it was only with this that he deprived some people of their jobs.

Subordinate of a workaholic

In fast motion: job offer as public supervisor in a renowned hotel, application form filled in and

2 days later: interview date,

2 days later: trial work day,

7 days later: acceptance of the job with contract documents in the email inbox,

9 days later: 8-hour introductory program/internal training,

5 days later: Start of work.

1st working day: Welcome of the housekeeper, team introduction by the housekeeper, induction of the trainee, meeting and walk-through with the housekeeper, introduction in the different departments.

2nd working day: service provider meeting, team meeting daily planning, introduction of the trainee, team meeting with housekeeper team

3rd working day: service provider meeting, team meeting daily planning, independent work with own team, team meeting with housekeeper team

4th working day: service provider meeting, team meeting day planning, own team meeting, getting to know the deputy supervisors, independent working with own team, team meeting with own team, team meeting with housekeeper team

5th working day: service provider meeting, team meeting daily planning, own team meeting, independent working with own team, team meeting with own team, team meeting with housekeeper team

So many meetings were not necessary, but demanded by the "authorities".

The trainee employee was exploited. He had to take responsibility even though it was beyond his capabilities. The instruction to train me came from the boss, what was he supposed to do? We were both overwhelmed on the first day.

Cooperation with all departments was assumed; this had already been communicated in the orientation program. There is nothing to be said against it, and it is required in almost all industries. I quickly discovered that no one wanted to work with the housekeeper team, in which I managed a small department.

If the personnel manager of a complete work area, who has only 2 mini-departments, including a deputy housekeeper (directly subordinate), forewoman service (contractor employee), 1 public supervisor (responsible for the public hotel area) and 5 housekeepers (control of the hotel rooms after cleaning), under her command (the best expression for it), is not able to lead these employees, then she should just make room.

There was yelling, raving, insulting, and I hadn't been there three days yet.

It started with the service provider team. They did not work accurately enough, everywhere still dirt, no order and the best: a "best worker" was introduced, where every week a champion was proclaimed. Nobody got anything special for it, just a "well done".

I was there and saw how many employees rolled their eyes and if they didn't have to work, they would have just left. The forewoman of this team had her hands full with keeping the mood and the team dynamics going, every day.

The housekeeping team meetings went the way of everyone saying what needed to be done, then walking out of the office. I prepared day-by-day work schedules so that I learned what was required and everyone knew what tasks needed to be done. Since we were still on call from the various departments in the hotel, I didn't give any timelines, but asked in the afternoon meeting what was still open. Then, as a team, we completed the tasks together.

I put a lot of emphasis on communication, and the team got used to that very quickly.

The deputy housekeeper also suffered under our boss. She sometimes had the task of sorting or reorganizing papers. Rooms were to be redecorated and old things disposed of. Basically, we were hired just to clean up. Sometimes we would meet during the break and she would tell me about it. Although she was my supervisor, I had the impression that she needed someone to have a good cry with. We had started at the same time, and I knew what she was talking about.

The laundry store, which I was additionally in charge of, was also a battlefield. When I had time, I cleaned it up. Folders also had to be created and papers sorted out. I reorganized the entire wardrobe because everything was in a mess. We had very long days at the hotel and it took forever until we had some structure in the affairs.

One employee from the service provider team was given hope by the housekeeper that he would get a contract with the hotel. He was to transfer to the housekeeping team. The contract just needed to be finalized and then things should start soon.

I heard about this on my first day. He never got that employment. He was a polite young man, with a lot of verve and fun at work. But when someone else was brought onto the team, he became incompatible. I had a conversation with his boss. She didn't know him that way either. When she told me that she could understand his behavior, she agreed. This is not how a manager should deal with people.

I had, as mentioned, more and more tasks thrown at me by my boss. I took part in meetings that had to do with events. Supposedly, that was my area of responsibility. From my department came a cleaner who was supposed to keep the sanitary facilities tidy. A circular email was always sent on the topics, I could have read it the next morning.

Then daily reassignment of the rooms, what do I have to do with that? She used to do that too, so now I do too. Ah, yes, the housekeeper wasn't a specialist at all, and she only learned personnel management in this hotel. So that's where the wind was blowing.

I asked her why there were so many chewing gum remnants on the floor in the outdoor area. Or why the very large outdoor lamps had never been cleaned. I did not get an answer. Three minutes before closing time, the housekeeper remembered that this would have to be done today. I told her that all my team members had completed their duty time and we would take care of it one by one starting the next day. I left the office and we did the task for the first time since the hotel existed (about 5 years).

A restaurant manager of the hotel asked me to come to his place because he needed a solution to cover a bar section. I went, saw what we could do, helped with the solution and everyone was happy. Only my house dame wasn't, as that wasn't my job.

Material ordering, linen stock, invoice control and hygiene stock were logical work processes for me. My team was also supposed to do all the clean-up work alone. The housekeepers sometimes loitered around for hours because they had to wait until the rooms were cleaned. The housekeeping team had nothing to do with that. The public team was allowed to slave away.

For the laundry cleaning we had a contract with a service company. I don't remember how many discussions I had with the housekeeper about allegedly inadequate service. When I spoke with the owner or had his employee on the phone, I was always friendly, the owner did not have to take the blame for my irritable mood.

Another point of contention was that the beds were stripped and clothes simply disappeared. Since I was responsible for the laundry, I had to take care of it. The housekeeper didn't think it was funny and let everyone know.

It got to the point where a garment of a guest was lying with me in the department. I was off duty and no one cared. This is a "matter for the boss" and the statement of my team members was correct, because my substitute was the house lady or her deputy. There was a row because this part was supposed to be cleaned and the guest wanted to leave in the afternoon. He came from another continent and they didn't want to have to send it behind. The owner of the laundry really went out of his way when I asked him for the favor of picking up the garment and returning it in the afternoon. I owed him one, he took me at my word. The end of the story, the guest had decided to stay longer after all. I was even made responsible for operational processes, although I had a day off.

I realized that I was the doormat of the housekeeper, and because of her behavior, no one really wanted to work with her. Even when there was a burst water pipe in the basement, most of the colleagues from the other departments refused to move materials, carpets and shelves so that we could remove the masses of water. It was only at the behest of the hotel director that everyone came flying in.

I had already mentioned that she regularly became loud and argued insultingly. Today I know that she was overwhelmed. She had stopped realizing how mean she had been to other people. In addition, she had never learned the basic rules of leadership. One by one, employees from her department left the hotel. I was still in contact with the forewoman of the service company later. She went to the neighboring hotel with part of her team. One member of the housekeeper team is now the housekeeper manager, there is no longer a housekeeper and some of the managers have been replaced.

I had already mentioned that she regularly became loud and argued insultingly. Today I know that she was overwhelmed. She had stopped realizing how mean she had been to other people. In addition, she had never learned the basic rules of leadership. One by one, employees from her department had left the hotel. I was still in contact with the forewoman of the service provider company later. She went to the neighboring hotel with part of her team. A member of the housekeeper team is now the housekeeper manager, there is no longer a housekeeper and some of the managers have also been replaced.

My services were also no longer needed. It was a nice place to work, even though my boss didn't understand how to deal with employees.

From the rain to the eaves

There are phases in life that have a beginning and usually no good end. My favorite experience, of lack of team leadership, is how I came to work for a company that had no idea of the craft that was being offered.

I was recruited as a forewoman in a hotel company and I entered, naively, a company that is a big player in France in the security industry. I never found out why she got into the cleaning business. They had participated in the tender of that time and won.

The buildings were reasonably well staffed, material was probably already in the building and work was already being done. Satisfactory? Certainly not, but one knows it, a certain goodwill is always given in the first days, the new service provider. I joined four weeks after the opening.

The area manager had no idea about the trades. A responsible property management was still being sought, so was in the works, ok! The team was taken over from the previous company, did their work as usual.

My area of responsibility was clear, every day I had to divide up the teams, check the materials, check the hotel rooms, keep track of the working hours, dress code and key management. But how clearly had the area of responsibility in my team been defined in advance? They worked in chaos for four weeks, just managing their own program, everything else was left to the forewoman, who made it clear after a short time that she no longer wanted this position. She was so privately connected to the team that she was unable to delegate tasks and was afraid that she would then no longer be liked. It can really become a vicious cycle.

Material had been brought on site sufficiently for the time being. The supply came into the hesitation and on inquiry I was put off again and again. The team's question about what to work with was justified, but I couldn't answer it. The area manager had probably placed an order, unfortunately it did not arrive with us.

Now I re-evaluated the goals and tasks were newly (better differently) distributed.

This was difficult to implement, because no understanding for the alleged additional tasks came up. I had been given the precinct plans, set up weekly work assignments and discussed them with the team.

All of them explained that they were not paid until the room cleaning was completed, that they were now to work on hourly wages, and that they were then to do the work for which an extra team had previously come, which had been commissioned by the previous company. No one had explained to them that this service now had to be done by the housekeeping team.

I understood the ladies, yet I delegated the tasks and they were done snarling.

The customer was very service oriented. A regular meeting was held with my supervisor. The result was satisfactory, we were doing a good job, they said.

Even though the customer was naturally skeptical, we developed a good rapport, so that she delivered the criticisms and praise to my team personally. Praise was so incredibly good for my team. I think that all positive news used to be put into their own pockets.

And then a new property manager joined the team, not with the necessary industry knowledge, but she had already been a property manager with experience in another area, which is why she was given this property, among others, there is no difference, according to the permanent area manager. I did not know whether I should cry or laugh. The customer could also only shake her head.

In addition, there were the extraordinary quality controls carried out by the plant management.

The team became restless, the material was not delivered, I introduced morning meetings, checked and retrained and tried to break old work patterns.

The work became more and more and we did not get any reinforcement, although I had urgently asked for it. Work was simply left undone, the contractually agreed working hours were not kept, the customer became dissatisfied, and I was left completely alone with all this.

When I was out of sight of my team members for a longer period of time, she had simply called it a day.

It got really bad when the wages weren't right, the pay slips were a long time coming and the work contracts were still not ready. My team had the feeling that they could not rely on anyone, especially since my efforts bounced off the new property manager and the area manager was supposedly no longer responsible for us.

One day, the customer asked me for a four-way meeting and asked me how I would evaluate the situation. She had the feeling that the management would not take care of this object seriously enough. She also told me that my team complained about the way the new company treated its employees. She had also heard about the unfinished documents and incorrect invoices. I was gripped by sheer horror. I could only promise to talk to the management.

Basically, I could understand the disloyalty. The team was just pushed around as if it was worth nothing. From my experience, they should have been talked to much earlier. In retrospect, I couldn't expect any trust and I didn't get it either, since no one on the upper floor was interested in my concerns.

On a very busy day, we got support from team members from another hotel. I was out with my teams in the departments because I knew every hand was needed. The property manager had taken control with a colleague. Since I hadn't seen everything, I wondered about a conversation that the other team started before we went into closing time.

The speaker complained about the behavior of the object manager and her colleagues. I guess they didn't understand the situation, didn't do their jobs properly, and "just hung around." She complained about the fact that everyone pitched in, only the two of them were probably too fine for it. I have to mention that the substitute team was also from the trade and could judge this. During this conversation, which I had only followed, I had inwardly resigned.

When the customer demanded that all housekeepers wear hairnets, she blew the entire team apart with it. Some didn't care, she was at work after all, others didn't want that at all. I never thought that the mood could get worse, I was extremely wrong. When I told my supervisor about this, she said that the customer was allowed to do this. She didn't care what the team members thought. For her it was only important that no complaints reached her. I was the gap between the management, the customer and the staff.

And then came what had to come. I was at the room inspection and when I went to look for my team, I found myself alone in the building one afternoon with mistakes and an unclean way of working. My entire team had not finished their work and had simply left. In horror, I called my property manager. She showed up at some point and saw what had happened. The next day she came back with warnings for the people concerned. As a result, three team members arranged to go on sick leave. I realized that I had lost.

Since I was not authorized to put together an independent team, I was anxious about every single person who got a job. Some came for a few days only to see that the job was not what they were promised, others stayed a few days longer because they needed the job.

I made sure that they had a good induction, took care of a good distribution of the tasks and thus made sure that the overtime, which kept coming up, was reduced. Things went quite well for a while, until it leaked out that we would not make it through the probationary period.

After several discussions with superiors, suggestions for improving working methods and attempts at restructuring, I had myself transferred. A replacement was found quickly.

Until I was transferred, we still didn't have employment contracts, payments were still incorrect, billing was always late, and the eternal promises that weren't kept didn't stop.

Short and sweet

Unbelievable ruthlessness awaited me in the next story.

My working time was divided into two sections, so I had an hour break that I could put to good use. I got myself a coffee, when the weather was nice I could sit outside in the park, and when it wasn't so nice I had a corner to myself in the building where I could read or listen to music.

Little by little the team arrived and we got coffee from the canteen and usually sandwiches or pastries that were left over. We then sat together for a few minutes and planned the afternoon. Since I was new to this team, I wanted to strengthen cooperation and promote communication. This was very important in this case, as there were several steps to be taken. The team coordinated itself independently and didn't waste any time, so everyone could finish on time.

Unfortunately, I have to mention that also in this case the team was taken over by the previous company and was misinformed by the management, which also had no service instructions on file. I am of the opinion, with intention, otherwise nobody would have remained in this object. The tasks in this house were still the same, only here, too, they were paid differently or not paid at all.

For example, in the outdoor area the umbrellas were closed and the tables were cleaned. For this the employee of the old company received in this case 10 € extra per day. This also only had to be done in the summer months. The new company offered this work step in the contract for the customer inclusive and the extra payment remained. The employee asked me after she got her pay if this was forgotten and when I inquired about it, I unfortunately had to tell her that it was included in the pay. She was furious about it and refused to continue this activity. I passed this on to the management, explained why the employee was angry and the matter was swept under the table. Since I only had the authority to look after the way the team was working and my property manager ignored me, I could do nothing but ask to speak to the management when the customer asked why we were no longer cleaning the outside areas.

The next day my property manager came and forbade me to talk to the customer. Everything that was operational and contractual was only allowed to go through her. I was only allowed to wish her a "nice end to the day". Any points of criticism had to be passed on directly to her or the management.

The customer also approached me about this because they preferred the direct communication channel and were not used to contacting the management. I explained what was being asked of me and shrugged my shoulders. In my opinion, it is easier to work together if you talk directly, so that problems can be dealt with quickly and the customer sees a good result very quickly, but I was told to keep quiet.

Another employee was appointed as forewoman before I arrived, but she had never received such an explicit formulation in writing. She carried the responsibility until I arrived and was never paid accordingly.

There were also no work contracts in this object yet. Somehow, I had the suspicion that too few office staff had too many tasks, because after months they still hadn't signed anything and there were some in the team who absolutely needed them. Be it for child support applications, housing subsidies, for submission to the employment office or whatever. I called my property manager and told her about the problems. At some point, she simply got out of my way.

When an employee came to me and had not received any pay at all, it turned out that her enrollment paperwork had been lost. She had to submit everything again. The fact that she came to work at all was a miracle to me. I know of incidents where employees just stopped showing up.

It also happened that the pay stubs didn't match the hours. Since my property manager had had enough of my persistence, I was ordered to the payroll office, to a lady who was responsible for accounting. I had previously collected all the timesheets so that we could compare the times. All team members received a hefty back pay.

I got to know other colleagues in my position through this job and asked if they also had such difficulties and they all said yes. I also got to know the team leader from the foremen. I didn't even know that we had such a position.

She offered me to run all material orders through her, since she had the material issue under her. I was happy with this encounter, as it made it so much easier for me to get enough material.

I assisted a fellow foreman from the hotel with the material deliveries, who was happy to have this information. He told me that he now also had problems with his team. The pay was not right and some colleagues had taken sick leave. He was going down with his department and didn't know how to do the work anymore. Since I couldn't offer him any help, I gave him the phone number of the forewoman who was responsible for us. Later I heard that this company had lost the entire contract in the hotel during the contract trial period. The team of the then colleagues gradually disbanded, they had enough of the eternal back and forth.

After a while, the customer of the plant decided to introduce quality controls, which were to be worked through in stages. I was responsible for the first stage, a colleague hired especially for this work for the second stage, and a control team provided by the customer for the third stage.

I was given an electronic control device that displayed the first stage. This also included the final inspection, which I was supposed to do at the end of the day, according to my supervisor. No, I didn't have to be on site for that, none of us would work that long. And, of course, the signature must not be missing.

For me, this meant taking my work equipment in hand during my free time and blindly working through all the points. All those who were familiar with this task did it from home or took the working materials with them to their free time.

I brought in the following example: A concert evening of my favorite band, admission 6.30 p.m., start of the event 8 p.m. The answer: "Then go out and finish the controls obligingly!" That meant I was supposed to have my work cell phone and the electronic control device with me at all times (the work cell phone was linked to the control device).

I did not have my work cell phone or any other work materials with me during my free time. I had not signed a contract for continuous duty or standby duty. I have nothing against overtime, sometimes I expect it from my teams. By the way, the longest overtime I worked in this branch was forty-five minutes and that was unique.

The next thing is that the client expected not only documentation, but also a signature to confirm the accuracy of the data provided. If there was any damage in the building, the documentation would show who was supposedly the last person in the building. Nobody in the management wanted to know about the consequences that I would have had to bear.

The arc in this matter was overstretched when I made a check during the day and noted that an area could not be cleaned because the equipment for it was missing. I entered this into the device and promptly received a call from the employee who was responsible for the second stage.

I was not allowed to make such a statement. I was supposed to set everything to green, even if it was not clean. When I, in this conversation, pointed out the signature to be provided, I was summarily sent on vacation and then dismissed. That went over neatly, I was still in the probationary period.

Unfortunately, I had to learn that a job title is worth more than sufficient knowledge. My former property manager had made a career for herself through her mother, and there was no trace of an independent way of working. She was not interested in the psychological strain on her teams. Stunned and saddened, I handed over my work equipment and never spoke a word to the people in charge again. I supported some of my team colleagues and coached them again and again. I hope that they have found their way and will continue to do so.

Cold water

A work briefing of three days. Good, the team was a team, well-rehearsed, competent, hard-working, with good communication skills and motivated.

The tasks were extensive, from preparations for the day shift to timekeeping for the teams, calling out instructions, replenishing materials, and keeping track of the individual work steps - everything a foreman has to do. Oh yes, the cleaning trolleys must also be left tidy, somehow this had to be mentioned again and again. The day shift didn't fare any better, they kept talking and talking. But well, at the end there was still laughter and cheerful waving goodbye.

It was supposed to be a full-time job. But first I got a mini-job contract, because I had another job. It was a good condition to get used to the job, since the concert hall was not yet fully booked. For the day, where it should really start, a team member was still searched and one wanted to quiet good training work. That also worked out.

I got my own compartment in the office in a re-gal with a small box. A service card was already prepared and the office key was given to me. Now and then I also like to lose things, so I put everything in this box after work.

There is nothing to criticize about the work itself, I was very happy for a short time. Only then came the day when my contract was to be extended and I almost fainted.

After reading through the sheet of paper that was supposed to be my work contract, I called the day shift and asked if it was nor-mal to get an incomplete and not agreed contract. Maybe someone simply under-wrote for fun, but that would also be seen in the performance. I argued with my short-term colleague and explained that I would not accept the job. My marginal employment contract was expiring and I wasn't going to sign the new one.

She couldn't help the situation because the real crap was coming from the management floor. But I didn't want to be pressed into such a system, I can't work with that and I could already imagine what negative rat-tail that would entail.

The mini-job contract became a part-time contract, with no fixed monthly working hours. The extension was given until the end of the probationary period. The note was not even properly formulated, one illegality after the other.

As I mentioned, everything was fine on the spot, but the office was of the opinion that the employees should not be taken seriously.

I complained to the works council about the way they were trying to pull the wool over my eyes, and unfortunately received no response.

Wages and payroll, as well as the registration and deregistration forms were sent to me by mail, on time and with the correct remuneration.

Unfortunately, there are always such deep black sheep, which should be increasingly controlled by the state organs.

As I mentioned, everything was great on the spot, only the office was probably of the opinion that the employees should not be taken seriously. I complained to the works council about the way they were trying to pull the wool over my eyes, and unfortunately received no response. Unfortunately, there are always such deep-black sheep, which should be controlled more by the state organs.

The dear predecessors

An application led to an interview, which went well. A day was chosen when I could go along to see what my future workplace might look like. Normally, this is not how it should be done. Since I didn't have a car to drive myself at that time, the area manager picked me up and we spent a day in schools, fire stations, kindergartens and social institutions.

And indeed, a few days later, she accepted me by phone for the position of property manager.

The contract came by e-mail, a telephone number of the secretary, so that I could go through and sign the documents with her. All documents were emailed to the head office, I received the confirmation and could celebrate the coming new year.

And it started. I received my car, my documents and an insight into a computer program. After finishing some more paperwork with the secretary, I drove home in the evening. I knew that the week would be a busy one, and just looking at the documents gave me an idea of what was to come.

For one week I was accompanied by the division manager. She showed me the properties I had to look after. I printed out the district plans and used them to orient myself. I talked to the teams on site and got an idea of the situation. If there were any decisions to be made, the area manager would take care of them. We discussed the situations and I took notes.

That was my initial training, then I was on my own.

The only thing that was stupid was that I worked for two weeks, then went to headquarters for five days to take part in the training, then worked for ten days and had four days of training again. You can't build up a bond like that. But well, if it was planned that way, it also had advantages. Then I had the training programs offered behind me.

Since we didn't always work in the office, at one point I met a colleague who handed me a burlap bag. "Your legacy." That was all. I looked inside and saw keys, a lot of keys, and when I wanted to ask what it was all for, the colleague was already driving off the yard. The area manager just said that we would create a key list, but not now, she didn't have time for that now.

I packed the bag into my car and for each key its lock was found. A list was ready long ago, when this became a topic again.

In the first time I got to know the teams, introduced myself to the janitors, invited the customer for a talk and got acquainted with the chief of the fire department. It wasn't pretty. People kept asking me how long I wanted to stay. I found out that I was already the seventh property manager for this area in three years.

Basically, they were just waiting for me to stop showing up once I'd been in the office for a day or two. I saw that in many an astonished reaction when I ran into the building managers or the customer.

I told about it in the office and heard some stories about my predecessors that were really scary. My boss told me that this area was difficult and that's why most of them left or got transferred. He promised me all the support I needed. I needed a plan to finally bring peace to the area.

At first, I completely ignored the building managers. I only talked to them when I ran into them or they called because something was wrong. I took care of my teams, encouraged them in what they were doing, got materials that hadn't worked in the past, took care of billing, there was still lost wages, and I offered them a personal level so that they would also tell me in confidence some of the things that were bothering them at work.

I rearranged rosters so that no one had to work overtime anymore. Then I took another look at the precinct schedules and realized that work was being done incorrectly. I made appointments with the customer who welcomed me into the office and we puzzled the schedules apart. I had him explain the timelines to me in detail. None of my colleagues was in a position to do this because they didn't want to or couldn't deal with it.

The next appointment was at a school. I explained to a principal and the janitor the schedules that came from the customer and asked them to deal with him if they were not satisfied with the performance. My teams were now doing wonderfully with their work schedules and the complaints were fewer. They had actually contacted the customer, who once again confirmed everything that I had already recounted.

There were job changes and I had to part with employees who did not fit into the work environment. Instead, I hired new employees, who quickly became part of the teams or became involved in the teams.

Little by little, the janitors began to trust me because they saw that I was there for my teams, reordering materials and taking care of equipment repairs. We talked about changes, times gone by, laughed and helped each other when the situation demanded it.

Then came the time of tenders and we lost all the objects in this constellation to the competition.

When I learned about this, I prepared my teams to change companies. I couldn't take anyone with me, but I could make sure they were taken over if they wanted to be. I had long conversations, said goodbye to them and wished them all the best.

Time witnesses

Six weeks before the end of the contract and the simultaneous new start, I sat with the work planner (yes, that was his job title) in the conference room and went through the time schedule for moving out of the old objects and moving into the new ones.

He wanted to organize 90%, leaving 10% for me. The complete management team was scheduled, material was to be ordered for the new objects, the moving team was organized, existing material was to be moved to the new objects.

I only had to take care of existing teams and the new team members and make a stock list so that he could buy and either make the contractual documents myself or have them made.

That was the plan.

Our boss always wanted to be on top of things, if help was needed he would be right there.

Big words.

The colleagues told me that they all had experience with restarts and handovers. I could come to them anytime.

Great offers.

When it was announced that we were going to lose all the properties, I went to my teams and prepared them. I asked them once I had the new tasks and templates, we would sit down and discuss if and how we wanted to work in the future. I knew from some team members that they had been in the properties for a long time and very likely did not want to change jobs. This made me sad, but understood that they wanted to stay.

I finished the inventory list and the work planner suggested that we make appointments for the object inspections so that we could have a look around. I prepared that as well and we set off. Everything went like clockwork until the thread broke.

After all the figures were in, the scope of the extracts had been clarified and the green light had been given by the head office, none of the colleagues had any more time.

In the meantime, a final cleaning of the building was to be completed. The work planner was supposed to take care of it, since he was the substitute for a colleague who was on vacation. He handed everything over to the authorized signatory. I got the job back from him and took care of the basic cleaning team myself so that we could hand over the building on time. This was a time-consuming task that I had not considered.

The work planner could not be found a short time later. I learned that he had to go into quarantine. My boss was in another precinct, also not always available. One colleague, as mentioned, was on vacation. The other colleagues moaned that they were drowning in work, and I was often told that there was still time, that I shouldn't be nervous.

We still had three weeks until the changeover and I was repeatedly put off with my concerns. Another training session was held. I attended one day and thought that was it. No, the second day still had to be added.

After the training sessions, I went to my properties and checked on my teams. From experience, I knew that by the end of a job, they were not working properly. In my case I was lucky, no one was on sick leave either, which happens very often. I could count on everyone really working until the last day.

A big praise came from the people in charge of the building. For most of them, this was not their first change of company. We talked through the last day of work, I made notes and passed them on to my boss, who was back.

My company car had to be exchanged because the leasing contract expired. I wasted another two days driving to the head office to change my company car.

I had noted in the inventory that a lot of junk had accumulated. We were still able to work with it, but there was a lot in the cleaning chambers that had not been picked up even after I had asked the responsible department to do so a long time ago. I got clear words for it from the work preparer: "With respect, this is not your decision." All right, with that sentence I was out of the act.

I asked my colleagues for support. I couldn't keep up with the writing of the new contracts. Supposedly, it wasn't that important, it could be done later. The only thing that would be important would be the registrations with the payroll department. I knew better and also got the confirmation from the payroll department and my boss. He sent a circular mail to all team members that it was now necessary to help. A colleague replied to this mail.

They would have offered help again and again, only I would not have accepted it. I was stunned. One morning I met this colleague and talked to her. She wanted me to know that the team spirit in this company was not so good and she just had to vent, especially since she was suffocating in her own work and was also no longer the youngest. At the end of the conversation, it was clear to me that she didn't care about anything if she wasn't the center of attention.

I talked to the legal department about termination notices and their deadlines. These had to go out as soon as possible.

The payroll department sent me a list that a legal employment contract needed, so that I would not forget anything. The new employees had to be entered into the payroll program, and new schedules had to be written so that everyone knew where they were going on the day they started. And my day also only had twenty-four hours.

My colleague came back from vacation and threw her hands up in horror. She reproached me for supposedly not accepting help. She wasted no time and immediately drove with me to my area. Far away from the office, I told her what happened during the time she was on vacation. She rolled her eyes, she also knew the game with this colleague. We telephoned for a long time with the work planner, made new plans and hoped that in the end everything would go well.

A jolt went through the whole company, because our boss again demanded teamwork.

A colleague wrote the contracts for me and sent them to the payroll office after they were signed. We talked on the phone when something was unclear and sent emails to each other for confirmation.

I assigned the other colleagues to the new objects so that the teams or individual co-workers were welcomed and filled out the forms that were needed.

The work planner was on site with the moving team for two days to guide them. When he saw the mess and how much needed to come out of the area, he just shook his head and regretted not sending a team to clean up sooner.

I took care of handing over the keys to the old properties and said goodbye to my teams.

We had a rally point, also for the material that remained, and we met there again around evening. I thanked everyone for their help and we parted ways for a while.

For me it was important to train the new teams, to get to know the new objects, to get in contact with the new employees responsible for the objects and to do the rest of the paperwork. At the end of the week, I met many colleagues in the office and we talked about the past days.

It always hurts when opinions diverge so much and you are held responsible for everything that didn't go well. I had to listen to a lot of criticism. So many things could have been done differently and help had been offered again and again. I remained calm, listened to what was said and drew a line under the matter.

My boss and I analyzed the actions of the last few days in a four-way discussion and agreed to do things differently next time. We had both learned from the experience.

The end of the story: Because of bad numbers and several losses of some orders, my job was eliminated and my territory was redistributed. I was the last to come and the first to go. The bitter part was that I couldn't say goodbye to my teams and was immediately let go. My company cell phone was taken away from me, so I couldn't even inform anyone about the leadership change. For sure, I didn't want anyone to lose their job or quit, I just had the feeling that the trust I had built up should not be completely destroyed, the trust of the teams was already destroyed again (there was such a great team dynamics) and the meanwhile much better reputation of the company should be maintained.

I was helpless in the face of all this.

Conclusion:

When I read over the written lines, I sometimes ask myself why I did so much to myself. I could have remained a simple employee and worked only on instructions.

I wanted to make a career, to make some changes in the world of work. It always bothered me to follow instructions that didn't make sense.

My school was not easy, sometimes desperate but also fun. As long as my path still has surprises and fun to offer, I'm happy to continue.

The more I think about it, the more I would like to convey to HR managers that they should be responsible for teams or employees, no matter what industry or level, and how lucrative it is to keep teams together. For my understanding we talk too little about this

My advice:

You have a team you work with? Then treat them as equals. They contribute with experience in many areas. Especially if you are the new ones in a company, you can benefit from this experience. Not everything you see has to be turned inside out just because there's a breath of fresh air. Old things have already proven themselves.

Be friendly to your team members and take responsibility when you lead them. They are only human and many do their best to do a good job. They seek validation and a sense of purpose in what they do. Many are proud of their accomplishments and want to show it.

The time they spend working is their life time, they are very much allowed to sweeten it.

These people leave their homes every day, head to their jobs and start being productive for you. Certainly, the money they get for doing this is a great motivator, it's even nicer when they are happy to show up and know they are welcome.

A great day should be ahead of them or even just hours dedicated to the work they have been assigned. Time is an important factor that is limited, so make sure that is not wasted.

When you are on site, greet them by name, with a smile. Make them feel like they are a part of the big picture.

Whether it's a good or bad reason for your visit, the first thing to do is to signal that they are respected.

Ask about their well-being, then listen! There is nothing more superficial than asking, "How are you?" and then not wanting to know the answer.

Small talk is great and you really get to know people then.

So is asking, "How's it going?" The worst attitude for team members is to just walk away. Maybe they do have, important information that you then miss. If you don't have time right now, say that too. Come back to it later. It's not rude, and at least you're not insulting them.

What I want to say is: When you enter the room, don't behave as if you were a high nobleman who wants to inspect his subjects! I am sure that these times are definitely over, if there was such a thing at all.

At a job interview, for example, you introduce yourself as Mr. A or Mrs. A and are not announced by a court jester or a palace spokesman. The relationship between team leader and team is now at eye level and you talk "normally" with each other.

There will always be points of criticism, as well as communication problems. In one-on-one discussions, these points can be dealt with and resolved more effectively than in a group. Sometimes it is difficult for team members to speak or explain themselves in front of others. And, most importantly, don't make a team member "round" in front of the assembled team. In most cases, this goes wrong. By doing so, you may completely break a dynamic team, or you may never have a chance to build a stable team because of such actions.

Mistakes also happen in the management layers. If the situation demands it, then stand by it. It does not make you weak, but human. Communicate the situation, suggest improvements and listen when a suggestion comes from the team. This can be a good approach to a solution.

About me

I was a service provider in various professional positions. It was good for me to start small. Through education, training, continuing education and listening to my mentors, I have grown. Now it is time to share my knowledge.

My project

Miteinander-business.com

My goal is to convince your company that by educating and developing your employees, you will have a stronger connection to the company. Thereby you reduce your employment costs.

With individual programs I can

- ➢ impart new knowledge
- ➢ expand limited knowledge
- ➢ highlight forgotten knowledge

Adapted to the needs, I advise online or in the company.

www.ingramcontent.com/pod-product-compliance
Lightning Source LLC
Chambersburg PA
CBHW052330220526
45472CB00001B/359